Special pinky - Sweet SB

Once upon a time, in a small town surrounded by tall trees and wide fields, there lived a boy named Samir. Samir was a kind, curious, and imaginative boy who loved to read, draw, and explore the world around him. But Samir was secretly sad. Even though he had a warm smile and a heart full of dreams, he often felt like he didn't belong.

You see, Samir's skin was a rich, deep brown, and he practiced a religion that was different from most of the kids in his town. While everyone else celebrated certain holidays, Samir and his family celebrated others. He wore different clothes on special occasions and ate different foods at home. Sometimes, other kids didn't understand these differences, and they made Samir feel like he was too different to be their friend.

At school, Samir tried to join in with the other children, but their jokes and games sometimes made him feel out of place. They didn't mean to be unkind, but they didn't realize how their words could hurt. So, Samir spent many recesses alone, dreaming of a world where he could find people who understood him and shared his love for adventure.

CAMP FRIENDSHIP

He held onto those dreams and continued to be kind and curious. He read more books, drew more pictures, and explored new ideas. After the last day of school, day, his parents decided to take him to a summer camp far from their small town. The camp was called "Camp Friendship," and kids from all over the world attended.

When Samir arrived at Camp Friendship, he noticed something amazing. There were kids with all different shades of skin, wearing all kinds of clothes and speaking many languages.

Some kids celebrated the same holidays as Samir, and others had their own unique traditions. Everyone was different, but everyone was excited to learn about each other.

At first, Samir was shy. He worried that the other campers wouldn't understand him, just like the kids back home. But as the days passed, something wonderful happened. A girl named Maya, who loved to draw just like Samir, asked if she could see his sketches.

She was the first person who ever made Samir feel like he had a place. She was so kind, funny, and smart. They spent hours talking and sat down on a log on the shore of the lake. Maya and Samir decided to draw together and as they sat on the log sketching the sparkling lake.

Samir asked, "Do you ever feel like some people are meant to meet?"
Maya looked up from her drawing and smiled.
"I do. Like you and me. We understand each other in a special way."

Later that day, a boy named Leo, who shared Samir's love for exploring, invited him and Maya to join a hike in the woods. When they returned, a group of campers who practiced the same religion as Samir welcomed him to join their special celebrations.

For the first time in his life, Samir felt like he truly belonged. He didn't have to hide who he was or feel different in a bad way. Instead, his differences were celebrated, and he found friends who shared his passions and respected his beliefs.

Samir's heart swelled with happiness as he realized that the world was much bigger than his small town and that there were many people out there who understood and appreciated him just as he was.

At the end of camp, Samir's parents picked him up, and he said goodbye to all of his new friends. Samir stayed in touch with the friends he made at Camp Friendship, especially Maya. The two visited each other, shared stories, and supported one another through life's ups and downs.

Samir also met new people who became his favorite companions, each one adding something special to his life. He learned that the world was full of people who were kind and open-hearted, just waiting to meet someone like him.

Samir became filled with the love and friendships he had always dreamed of. He traveled to many places, met many more people, and always carried with him the lesson he learned at Camp Friendship: that it is okay to be different, and that he was not alone in feeling that way. Sometimes, it takes a little time to find your people.

And so, Samir's secret sadness faded away, replaced by the joy of knowing that he had found his place in the world—a place where he was loved, valued, and truly belonged. He couldn't wait for the next summer he could go to Camp Friendship.

About the author

Yusuf Saadat is a dedicated educator and the vice principal of a school in Seattle. With a deep passion for working with children, he is committed to helping students navigate the challenges of life and realize their full potential. Currently pursuing his Ed.D., Yusuf is devoted to continuous learning and growth, both as an educator and as a person. When he's not working with students, he enjoys staying active and spending time outdoors, appreciating the beauty of nature. Through his writing, Yusuf hopes to create stories that make kids feel seen, heard, and understood, inspiring them to believe in themselves and embrace their unique journeys.